These are some of the awarenesses
that have been helpful to us
                    in our practice.
We are grateful for them and
would like to share them with you.

It is handwritten so that it can
    be read slowly with the heart
    instead of quickly with the head.

We offer this book in loving-kindness.

A Center
for the Practice of
Zen Buddhist Meditation

Mountain View, California
July, 1984

THE KEY

and the Name of the Key
Is Willingness

Zen Center
POBox 91
Mountain View, CA 94042

Monastery/Retreat Center
POBox 1994
Murphys, CA 95247

A Center for the Practice of
Zen Buddhist Meditation
-publisher-

ISBN 0-9614754-0-4

Printed on recycled paper.

Please
do not do yourself the disservice
    of assuming
    that there is something to do
    that is more important
              than just being

right here
right now
present

aware
attentive
accepting.

1.

We spend our lives trying to alter externals,
trying to get what we want,
trying to manipulate the "whats".

Relationships, friends, lovers
money, possessions, values, opinions, ideas,
life, hopes, dreams, children, jobs,
death, education, etc.
are "whats".

Whats come and go.

Whats pass.

Whats are illusion.

Peace, joy, and freedom lie in
        real-izing
        the how,
        the process,
rather than the content of life.

We get so caught up in the specifics,
the "whats" of life, that we can't step
back and see the broader view,
    the whole, the process, how it is.

    We don't realize that
we experience our lives the way we do,
    not because they actually are that way,
    but because that's how we see them.

It's not what you do, it's how you do it.
It's not what you see, it's how you see it.
It's not what you think, it's how you think it.
It's not what you feel, it's how you feel it.

There is nothing wrong in the universe.

Wrong exists in our limited view
of the universe.

wrong\ rȯŋ\ n. [ME, fr. OE wrang] not the way
I want it
right\ rīt\ adj. [ME, fr. OE riht] the way I
think it should be
fair\ fa(ə)r\ adj. [ME fager, fair fr. OE] what
I want
good\ gud\ adj. [ME, fr. OE gōd] whatever
I like (at the moment)
bad\ bad\ adj. whatever I don't like
(at the moment)

These ideas that we have
about how things are
or how they should be
exist no where else
except in our own minds.

That voice inside your head
is not the voice of GOD.
It just sounds like it thinks it is.

4.

What are your definitions of the following words, not as defined by dictionary or society, but as you honestly experience them?

wrong
right
fair
good
bad
honest
selfish
need
want
security
enough
loving
equal

It is important to realize that these are your definitions and not everyone's.

Nothing needs to change.

You don't have to get better,
    you already are better.
If you think you can do better,
    do better.

Nothing real is stopping you.

The only thing stopping you
        is the thought,
            the belief,
that something is stopping you.

What stops you is inside, not outside.

Love anything. Hate anything.
The effect you have on the external
might be negligible,
the effect on you,
monumental.

When you get through with all
    this stuff,
    all these problems
(jobs, education, husband, wife, house,
  children, car payments, yardwork, bills),
    are you really going to be able
        to <u>live</u> ?!?

This stuff,
these problems,
<u>are</u> your life .

When you get through with all this,
you'll be through with all this,
that's all.

We're going so fast all the time,
racing frantically toward a time
when we can

        S

         L

          O

           W

             down.

When we've going so frantically,
with so much to do and so little time,
it never occurs to us
that what we really need to do is

9.

How do you feel when you
    slow down
    relax
    stop

How do you keep yourself from
    slowing down
    relaxing
    stopping

What kinds of things do you believe about life or yourself that stop you from being the person you want to be?

What do you tell yourself about who you are or who you should be, and how does that get in your way?

Being the fastest, the richest, the thinnest, the smartest on the treadmill won't prove anything.

There's nothing to prove,
nothing to win,
nothing to get.

The fact that someone else is right doesn't mean that you're wrong.
Perhaps you're both right.
Perhaps you're both wrong.
Perhaps you're both right and wrong.

What do you give up in order to fight this losing battle (to be bigger, stronger, smarter, righter, perfecter)?

The nuclear arms race is proof
that if anyone loses,
everyone loses.

No one wins unless everyone wins.

No one,

no thing,

can take your peace,

your joy,

your adequacy,

away from you.

You have to give it up
voluntarily.

And we give it up so easily,
for just about anything:

other people's opinions, late meals,
long lines, red lights

*!@☆?!

SCREECH!

13.

What you want to "become"
is inside you.

And you've already responding to it

or you wouldn't be reading things
like this.

The odds of anyone ever getting all
        or even most
of what s/he wants at any given time
        are very slim.

There are always
        irresponsible, late, rude, inept,
        stupid people;
a lack of
        parking places, appointments
        available, money, promotions,
        weekends, dates, affection, sex;
an excess of
        criticism, judgements, things
        spilled on clothes, unexpected
        guests, red lights ...

You have no choice about what you get.
You have absolute choice about what
                        you do.

When you're trying to get what you want
out of life

life can be very hard.

When you learn to want what you get
in your life

life can become very easy.

Instead of the common
"I want what I want when I want it;"
we learn to say,
"I want what I get when I get it."

I might not always like it.
And I always accept it.

What kinds of things do you give up your peace and joy for? Consider "life-time whats" like job or family or security, "current whats" like specific people or causes, "cosmic whats" like death or nuclear warfare and "mundane whats" like the store you're hurrying to is closed or you've just spilled something on your favorite pants.

Perhaps it would be helpful to make a list of these.

1) How do you determine what you want?

2) How do you feel/act when you get what you want?

3) How do you feel/act when you don't get what you want?

4) What do you give up in your life in order to cling to your preconceived notions about what you want?

IT IS MUCH EASIER
TO WANT WHAT YOU GET
THAN TO
GET WHAT YOU WANT.

When you want what you get,
you've always got what you want,
because you've always got what you get.

This is not to say
that we "shouldn't" have or do.

Remember:
There's no reason to do or not to do anything, and
it is the process, the how, we're concerned with,
not the content, the whats.

It's just that the process of wanting
is very different from having or doing.

It seems like wanting results in having or doing.
When we look more closely
we begin to see that wanting
actually only results in more wanting,
the increasingly demanding habit of wanting.

Having or doing the object of our wanting
satisfies only briefly and then
the wanting captures our attention again.

Remember: the 4 causes of suffering
• not getting what you want
• getting what you want and not being
satisfied with it
• being separated from those or that which
you love
• having to endure the company of those or
that which you do not love

They all actually say,
"not getting what we _want_."

We think that wanting
is the source of our satisfaction.
                              In fact,
it is the source of our dissatisfaction.

It is very important that we learn
               how we do wanting
               rather than believing
that we must get what we want.

First find the contentment,
               the joy,
               the peace where you are.
To do wanting is to believe
that you are lacking, inadequate.
The present moment lacks nothing.
The present moment is all that is.

First experience what is,
               what actually is,
not assuming that there's a lack,
then decide what, if anything,
               you could want.

23.

What is _IS_:

Could be, should be, ought to be,
might be, hope will be,
wish could be, want to be,
are postures we maintain
to avoid accepting what _IS_,

to remain ignore-ant
of what _IS_.

In this way we manage to avoid
the only time in which we live.

Our lives consist of
"what _IS_"
in the present moment.

"Should" is a stick we use
to beat ourselves with.

Nothing but the way it is

"could" ever be

or

"should" ever be.

THIS IS IT.

Anything else is just our
"better idea".

There is nothing wrong with the way
it is.

The only "wrong" is in our thinking,
in our believing

in our "better idea".

"Should"

is

illusion

fantasizing.

"Should" is "Never Never Land".
"Should" never has been and never will be.

When you stop comparing
what is right here and now
with
what you wish were,
you can begin to enjoy what is.

(You might as well enjoy it,
it's all you've got.)

And you don't really know for sure
that you don't want it
because
you've always been off looking
at how you'd rather life were.

If this is all we've got,
it's also the best we've got.

Why not enjoy it?

Remember:

Just because you don't like something
doesn't mean there's anything wrong with it.

It just means you don't like it.

A little secret between us —
  Regardless of what anyone might think
  about what IS,
                    it actually is perfect!

Until we learn to accept
we cling to things being
      the way they have been,
      or we wish they were,
      or want them to be,
      or hope they will be.

   We tense up all our muscles,
      dig in our heels,
      and RESIST.

   Then we believe that the energy
      we have put into resisting change
is actually maintaining the status quo.

      We actually begin to believe
      that we are holding things
         together.

Then we draw the conclusion: I am in control.
   And that conclusion is an illusion.

      When we learn to accept everything
         that comes into our lives,
            we are free from
         the pain of resistance.

Resistance does not work.

CHOICE #1:

You can accept

what is.

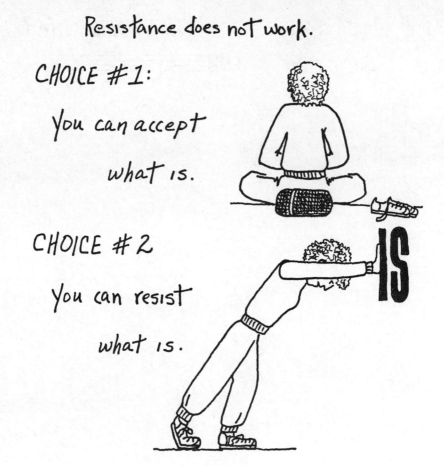

CHOICE #2

You can resist

what is.

Result of your effort: #1-none. #2-none, except your own suffering

What IS just is.

In acceptance there is peace.
In resistance there is pain.
The choice is always ours.
It is just that simple.
And no one ever said it was easy...

What are you resisting in your life?

YOU,
each moment,
contain all that is,
everything you seek.

When you know that,
when you "come from" that,
you see perfection and complete adequacy
all around you.

When you don't know that,
when you don't "come from" that,
you spend all your time trying to
manipulate externals so that you can
get whatever you think you need
to make you feel "enough".*

*That's known as adding legs to a
painted snake or putting another
head on the one you already have.

35.

SAY

TO LIFE

It is not necessary, or desirable,
to try to become someone
you think is better than the way you are.

Just be willing to find out
who (how) you really are.

You might be surprised to find
that when you let yourself be
who you really are,
not who you think you are,
or who you're afraid you are,
you really are quite an acceptable
person.

And with a little practice
you'll even realize that you are, in fact,
a love-able person.

The ways you think you are,
   not the ways you really are,
are the bars on your own personal prison.

Please recall:

Just because you think something is so
(that you're bad, selfish, ugly, perfect,
brilliant, superior, inadequate)
doesn't mean it's so.

It only means that you think it's so.

You are doing your life.

Not that you are responsible
in the sense that you are to blame
          or that you have caused it —
just that your reactions, responses,
feelings, thoughts, ideas, attitudes,
theories, standards, beliefs, likes,
dislikes, wants, needs, etc.
          are yours.

They create your world.

They are what you call "I" or "me."

And it is THIS
which you must face honestly
and learn to love and accept
     through compassion.

When we waste all our time
trying to be better,
trying to improve our "self,"
we're failing to make the only contribution
we'll ever be qualified to make —
our own.

You don't have to change anything.
Especially yourself.

You are the most perfect (and only!) you
ever produced.
Be content with that.

Idealizing about the perfect you
just wastes your precious opportunities

for a perfect NOW.

Sit back, close your eyes and let an image come to you of your "perfect self," the idealized you you wish you were or "should be". Picture what you and your life would be like.

Perfect Me

Now sit back, close your eyes and let an image come to you that represents your "worst self", the way you see yourself when you're "awful". Picture your view of yourself as the person you "shouldn't" be.

Awful Me

We maintain by resisting.

We maintain who we think we are
by resisting who we really are.

The more I cling to becoming "a better person,"
the more I resist who I am,
the more I stay stuck where I am.

When I say "YES," *
when I embrace however I am,
I've already changed.

The moment I let go
everything is different,
though probably nothing external changed.

(Consider where the change actually
occurred...
all I did was let go of my resistance.)

* If you can't say "YES!", you can probably
say "OK". It's a beginning.

45.

Now, sit back and close your eyes, take a couple of deep breaths and let an image come to you that reflects as clearly as possible how you really are. See yourself going about your daily life, doing what you do, thinking your thoughts, feeling your feelings...

Really Me

46.

Can you picture what your life would be
like if you accepted*it (if you loved it)
as it is?

Picture of my life
accepted as it is.

*Acceptance is not resignation.

Resignation happens
with your head
d
o
w
n

Acceptance happens   u
with your head
p

When you start being too successful,
   doing too well;
   getting too good
   at this process of letting go,
there's a good chance you'll lose interest.

                    Because if you really let go,
                         if you really accept,
                         you're going to change.

And there's a good chance that that's
the last thing you really want to do.

Say "YES!"

Simply meet each experience of life,
inside and out,
body, feelings and mind,
with all the love and acceptance
you can muster.

If you feel like you could love more,
love more!

If you think you might like to work on
your reactions,
appreciate yourself for being willing,
be grateful for the awareness,
and love yourself for caring.

Peace and joy
are what's there
when we stop doing

everything else.

"Then why do we keep doing this?"

There is surely a pay-off for maintaining
life as we know it (especially the horrors,
the shocking awfulnesses of our world).
What would we talk about without them?
What would be the daily news?
How would you know how lucky you are?

Wanting always to be
    right, good, strong,
    smart, successful,
    loving and rich

Is like wanting always to have
    summer,
    daytime, sunshine,
    warmth and 70°.

Not only is it impossible,
    it's boring.

Until we've accepted where we are
            in our own growth,
         we cannot go anywhere else.

      As long as we're attempting to
         get rid of something,
   we're insuring that it will be with us always.

      We will always be capable of everything
            (we are all-potential)

         When we accept that,
         we are free to choose
      what (how) we do.

         We are no longer driven
         to be only one way,
   i.e., good, right, strong, smart, etc.

   We can love ourselves when we've
               wrong as well as right,
               weak as well as strong,
               angry as well as peaceful.

         There is no such thing
         as a one-sided coin.

A little wise secret:

You don't need to know anything
in order to be wise.

All you need to do to be wise
is to accept.

You don't need to have anything
"figured out"
or "together".

Love as much as you can
from where you are
with what you've got.

That's the best you can ever do.

Remember: It's the process,
not the content,
that counts.

If how you're doing it
is total love and acceptance,
that's the wisest thing you can do.

It does no good to search frantically for peace, to seek anxiously after love or joy or freedom.

If you want to find joy, do joy.
If you want for there to be peace, do peace.

It is good to be a person of means.
If the end is never in sight
it doesn't matter.

We do what we do for the joy of doing, not because we're going to get a reward when it's over.*

* or the odds are real good that we'll be disappointed a lot.

We know what's right. We don't know
what's right for everyone or everything
(though sometimes we act as if we think
                    we do).
It's not necessary or desirable to know
   everything (or anything) for everybody.

     You know what's right for you
              each moment.
Not fun or pleasurable or exciting —
            just right.
     Deep down in your bones,
            in your insides,
            in your heart.
It may take some practice before you
   trust that you have that
            knowingness
      about everything,
              and
   if you pay attention,
   that knowingness
is already guiding you through your life.

    To the degree that you know it,
           do it.
Not because you "should" or you'd "better,"
    just because it feels good
   to do what you know is right!

Let yourself recall times when you knew inside what to do and you didn't do it, times when you followed your "head".

How did you feel?

Recall an occasion or occasions when you followed your intuitive knowing and did as your "heart" guided.

How did you feel?

Do you experience a difference in making a decision intuitively (heart) and rationally (head). What is that difference like for you?

58.

Magic formula:
    If you want to prove
        to yourself
    that you're a good person
    who doesn't need to be punished,
just choose to do what you know is right.

    If you want to continue to be unhappy,
        grab for the fleeting moments
    of whatever your heart is telling you
                aren't right for you
        so you can continue to see yourself
                    as a bad person.

When you're unhappy
about something you've done,
it's probably not because of what you've done
as much as that you didn't listen
to your heart
when it guided you not to do it.

Just do what you know is right.

You can do it for yourself
and as a gift to everyone else.

Do good
and feel good
and be happier
and more willing
and more loving
and more forgiving
and more accepting
and more compassionate
and the whole world will feel better.

When we are willing to let ourselves feel good,
   when we're ready to forgive ourselves
      for ancient crimes and sins
         (real and imagined)
      we begin to choose to do that
   which lets us feel good about ourselves.

         Not because we "should".
   We do what we do because it feels good,
         because we want to.

When it comes right down to it,
it doesn't really matter to us
what others think of us.

They criticize us and we've defensive.
They compliment us and we don't believe them.

      The only praise we really accept
         is from ourselves.

When <u>we</u> feel satisfied with what we've done,
                  we're pleased.

Doing good feels good.

If you don't want to feel good,
    don't do good.

"I'm too tired."
"I'm too busy."
"Who cares?"
"What difference does it make?"

None.

Except to the person doing good.
    That person is good.
    And it feels good.

Exercises:

1) Do a kindness for someone* everyday for one week.

2) Each evening before you go to sleep, be kind to yourself and remember all the good/kindness you have done that day. (Be sure to include compliments, smiles, kind words and thoughts.)

p.s. If you have a little voice inside who wants to tell you how you're not a kind person, just gently, lovingly remind that voice that you know she/he thinks that, and you're glad to have his/her opinion and you will listen in detail at another time. This ten minutes is devoted to doing good.

p.s.s. If you can stretch it to 15 or 20 or 30 minutes, do so. Focus on all the good done today by you and any and everyone else.

* Remember, you are a someone!

63.

Freedom lies in seeing
  how we do liking and disliking,

  not in getting
  all the things we like

  or in getting rid of
  all the things we dislike.

If you find something unacceptable,
draw a bigger circle of acceptance.

Just keep drawing a bigger circle
until nothing is excluded.

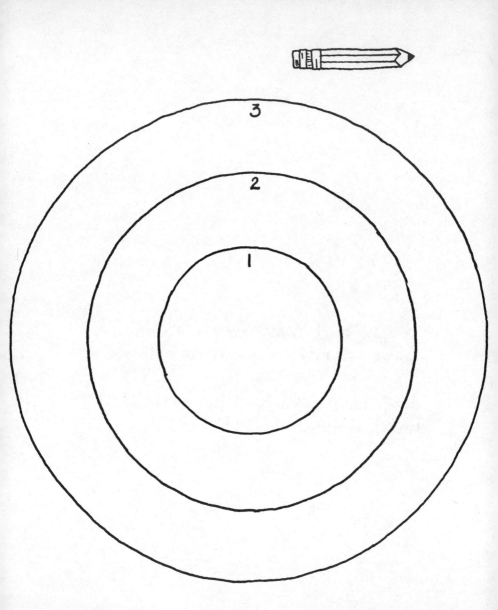

Consider what you can accept easily (1), what you're working on accepting (2), and what still seems completely unacceptable (3).

What I'm currently *experiencing
as unacceptable is...

*Check back in six months or a year and see if
all these "unacceptables" still seem unacceptable or if some are inside the circle of
acceptance.
67.

Remember:

You don't have to give up
the "unacceptables"—

you'll just suffer
with each one you cling to.

("Pushing away" and
"holding onto" are two sides of the same
coin. They are both clinging.)

And we do suffer
with each one we cling to.

Don't waste your time trying to change—
anything.
                    (You don't even know
who wants to change, or what you would
change, or what that change would
bring. You'd just be trading one opinion
for another.)

    Just draw a circle of acceptance
around everything in your awareness.
        Just say "yes".

You don't have to do anything about anything.
    Just let everything be as it is,
at least until you can see how you're doing it.

If you think you can feel better
by doing something else,
or being something else,
or being somewhere else,
then
feel better.

Don't be confused by thinking you need to
do something else,
or be something else,
or be somewhere else.

Just be content to
feel better.*

*It can save a great deal of time, energy
and money.

Whether life is seen
as an opportunity
or a burden
depends on one's point of view,
not on one's circumstances.

You have learned
to walk,
to talk,
to dress yourself,
to drive a car,
to prepare food,
to play a musical instrument?
to speak a foreign language?
to do all sorts of things that
in the beginning seemed insurmountable.

Because you wanted to.

71.

If you see a problem, it's yours.
If you think that somebody should do something,
remember that you're as much a somebody
as anybody.

Be what you want the world to be.

Stop fighting — you're the only one
standing between you and peace.

When you can let it be the way it is
and not how you've decided it should be,
you can begin to see that the only thing
making you unhappy
is your idea about how it should be.

Once you see that your idea
isn't "better" for anyone
but you,
you can begin to see other views,
then all views,
then what "views" really are.

All that is required
is that you accept
that which is totally unacceptable—to you.

There's a clue there. It says
"to you".
Not to everybody. Not to the world,
or society. Not to god. To ~~you~~.

That which is unacceptable to you
exists only through the power
which you give it.

If you stop making it a problem,
it ceases to be a problem.

All you must do
is accept
all
that is unacceptable to you.

You see,

we
push
our
own

buttons.

Our language misleads us because we say:
    "He is handsome."
    "The sunset is beautiful."
    "She is angry."
                                    rather than:
    "My experience of him is 'handsome'."
    "My experience of the sunset is 'beautiful'."
    "My experience of her is 'angry'."

"Is that always true? Can't I ever experience
something that isn't my experience,
                            that isn't mine?"
    Yes, it is always true.
    No, we can't experience anything
                    except our own experience.

It is very helpful in taking responsibility
    for ourselves and our lives
    to realize that our difficulties lie
    with our own experience,
    not with externals.

We want the externals
to be the cause of
who we are;

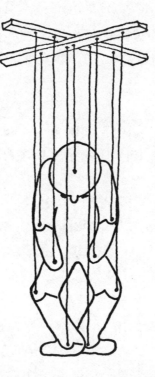

In fact, the externals
are the result of
who we are.

Seeing oneself as a victim is a choice, not a requirement. At any time, one can choose to be...

CLICK!

The entire world is a mirror.
The entire world is a mirror.

THE ONLY THING
YOU CAN EVER EXPERIENCE
IS YOURSELF.

You can only think your thoughts,
feel your feelings,
experience your experience.
You can never experience anyone else's.
Everything you think, feel, do, see is you.

Your thoughts, your feelings, your ideas,
your values, your philosophies, your
opinions, shape, mold, "create" your world.

Everything you experience is as it is
because that's how you experience it.*

*If an act occurs in a forest and there's no
"you" to experience it, would it occur?

Clue: What would it be without your per-
ceptions of shape, size, qualities, time,
color, intent, function, purpose, etc.?

80.

Projection
or
how we "create" the world we see

We experience the world (people, situations, things)
and instead of owning our own experience
we project our thoughts, feelings, values, etc.
into the "thing" (the "what").
Our projection might or might not be true
for the person or thing,
and it is always true
of the person experiencing it.

(Notice whose head it appeared in
and whose mouth it came out of!)

And have you ever noticed
We like to "give away" qualities
we experience as negative
and feel better,
while we tend to "give away" qualities
we experience as positive
and then feel lacking.

81.

Anytime we attempt to cling
to one side of a duality
we can know that we are clinging equally
                    to its opposite.
(Clinging and pushing away are the same.)

We hold onto someone we love,
    and they leave us.
We try to push something away from us,
    and we can't get rid of it.
We want only quiet, refined, intelligent
people around us. We are plagued by
    loud, rude, ignorant people.

Our standards have "created" both groups for us.

When we accept that both simply are
            sometimes this,
            sometimes that,
            we are free.

Once you know that what you're experiencing
is the result of how you are,
of how you experience,
of how you see the world,
you'll be less involved with trying to change
the content of your experience.

You live in the world you have chosen.

Your world continues to be the same,
not because that's the way the world is,
but because you continue
to make the same choices.

What you see
is who you are.*

* This glass is
  □ half full
  □ half empty
    84.

Anything that happens could be experienced
in millions of ways.

What happens is not important.

How we react to what happens
is very important.

It is not what we get that matters;
it is what we do that matters.

You can let go anytime you're willing.

There is no way to <u>get</u> love
or peace or joy or freedom
To <u>do</u> love and joy and freedom and peace
is the way.

The process, the means, is the point,
not the end.

If you really want to do it differently,
you're going to have to find the willingness
to stop punishing, criticizing, judging,
beating and otherwise "improving" yourself.

The way out of this mess
we've got ourselves into
is directly through the center.

We are free
the moment we are willing
to accept
ALL.

No resistance at all to anything
(including our own thoughts and feelings).

What is, is.

Many of us have learned to believe
we can "improve" ourselves
by a very cruel system
of self-rejection and abuse.

We call this the
"Building a Better World Through Hatred"
school of thought.
The slogan is,
"You, too, can hate yourself
into being a loving person."

The fact is that beating yourself
will never make you a better person.

If you're hating, you're doing/being hatred.

The only way to be loving
is to love.

There is nothing real in the universe
that requires you to hate.
Nothing real gives you permission to
or expects you to punish or reject or be cruel
(even to yourself!)

Beating yourself will never
make you a better person.

There is no excuse for not loving.
(And not loving is no excuse for beating yourself.)

Beating yourself is what keeps you from seeing
that there is no such thing as a person
who needs to be beaten!

You will never learn to be a loving person
through a process of hating.

Beating yourself
is a selfish and ego-centric act,
and your continuing to beat yourself
                    will insure your continued
                                        selfishness
                            and ego-centricity.

    Would you teach a child to love
by hating it, beating it, rejecting it?
    Or by lovingly guiding it
to experience its own inherent goodness?

We are all children
who can find
our own intrinsic goodness
that GOODNESS
that IS us through loving kindness.

GOODNESS

Exercise:

Some circumstances of life have made it necessary for you to be responsible for a newborn baby. Consider how you would like that baby's life experience to be, how you want him/her to grow up, what kind of adult you would like him/her to be. Write out all the things you'll do and ways you'll be in order to provide the best life experience for the baby.

Now begin to do those things
for yourself!!!

It seems that we are stuck
with needing to take responsibility
for being loving and accepting

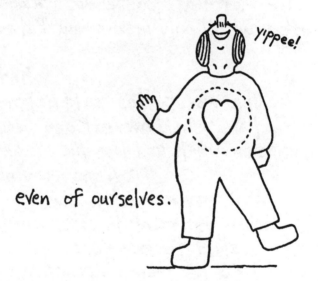

even of ourselves.

Perhaps if we stopped beating ourselves
there would be no reason to continue
the behavior that "leads" to the beating.
If you stopped beating yourself for overeating,
would you still want to overeat?
Please don't be too quick to believe
that you would eat everything in sight
until you burst.
(You've conditioned to think that.
The fact that you believe it doesn't mean
it's true. It only means you believe it.)

Find out.
The worst that could happen
is that you would overeat and beat yourself
and go on a diet and lose the weight you gained,
and you know how to do that.
AND maybe, just maybe
when you start to care about yourself,
start to love yourself,
to be there supporting yourself,
(not in an overinflated, egocentric sense,
just as a basically kind, caring, decent person
who wants to do good)
you won't want to hurt your body anymore.
Maybe you won't want to hate yourself
or suffer by feeling inadequate
and unattractive.

Feeling better about yourself
through compassion and acceptance
truly is not egocentric.

It is the first giant step
                    away from egocentricity.

        Being kind to yourself
        lets you be kinder to others —
and that just might be
the finest gift
you can give to the world.

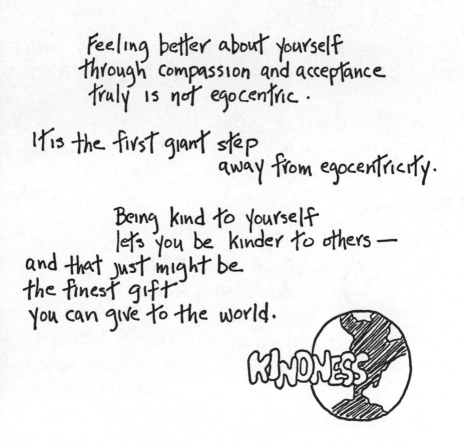

Egocentricity
or self-indulgence
or selfishness
means satisfying one small part of yourself
        whose desire is temporary and fleeting.

    It is possible to do
what is most compassionate for <u>all</u>.
(And we must remember to include ourselves
                        in that all.)

    Not indulging yourself does not mean
            never having an ice cream cone
                    or a new car,
        it means not always having
                    an ice cream cone
                or a new car
        everytime you want one.

There is a middle way that transcends
    always and never.

We continue to choose our old way,
the way that causes us to suffer
because it's familiar,
it's safe, it's comfortable .
We know how to do it,
and we know who we are when we're doing it.

No risks here.

Many of us have to be very miserable
before we'll risk the insecurity
of doing it differently;
of letting go of our ideas about
how life "should" be.

We find our willingness
to let go
when we have suffered enough...

We suffer because we cling. Suffering is
caused by our unwillingness to accept
what IS.

We suffer when:
   We don't get what we want.
   We get what we want and aren't
      satisfied with it.
   We are separated from those or
      that which we love.
   We are forced to endure the
      company of those or that
      which we do not love.

When we see
that the world we experience is created
by our own projections and postures
we realize there's nothing out there to hold onto.
If we believe there is
we have bought a bill of goods.

Getting everything in the world
doesn't protect us from suffering.
It could all be gone tomorrow. Today, even.

And just because you know this
doesn't mean you're any less safe
than you ever were.

Now you're sure how it really is.
No more reason to try to kid yourself.

There is no thing to hold onto.
Might as well relax.
Might as well let go.

Nothing will be any worse —
and it might just be
a whole lot better!

Just let go and fall...

UP!

There's no reason not to have it all.

You needn't waste your time
trying to get rid of
what you don't want in your life...

Just add what you do want.

If you think you'll be happier
if you're single or
if you have a new Rolls Royce
then
BE HAPPIER!!

Don't waste your time
trying to get rid of your mate
or trying to get a new car.

Add what you really want—
"HAPPIER".

Our relationship with others
is based on liking and disliking.
(More on disliking than liking, it would seem,
since of the people you have met
there are many more who are not in your life
than who are in your life.)

We keep looking for the things
we <u>don't</u> like about everything.

How it's different from me.
How it's "other".
How we're separate.

"Oh, I'm not like that." "I would never
do that." "I don't know how people
can be like that!" (Sure I do.
I'm seeing it, aren't I?)

The obvious conclusion of my judgments
is that, of course, my way is better.

I am different, better, superior.

And that separation causes our suffering.

There is no need,
no reason,
to make a contest out of anything.

It is not necessary to demand
that life be a certain way
and then be unhappy
when it's not.
It is not necessary
to be frustrated or angry
or anxious or sad.
People are,
but they don't have to be.

Unhappiness is not a requirement.
Those feelings are the result of wanting
something other than what is.

And if you find yourself suffering
because you've got something
you don't want...

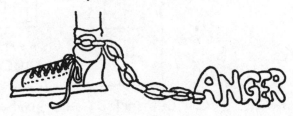

if you can feel love and compassion
for yourself
for suffering
you will cease to suffer.

When you love yourself in your unhappiness,
you are no longer unhappy,
you are loving.
We are not suffering when we are loving.

Remember JOY travels from the inside
to the outside.

Look for the joy
in every moment.

Exercise:
  See if you can find joy in doing
something you've told yourself is awful.

The problem is not with the "what",
          the thing,
          the external.
The problem is with us,
          with our own process of
          liking and disliking.

We literally like and dislike ourselves
          to death.
     (Stress is like/dislike.)

If you have to eat custard and custard
          is your very favorite in the
world, you're in heaven. If you have
to eat custard and you hate custard,
     despise it worse than anything,
     you're in hell, you're miserable.

The problem is not with the custard.

And it is much easier to see that
with custard than it is with the boss,
husband/wife, mother-in-law, the
government, etc. and no less true.

Suffering is not a requirement.
Letting go of liking/disliking
     is not a requirement.
It is simply a way to end suffering.

And you can know that as long as you
cling to a fixed idea of how life needs
to be, you are bound to suffer.
Because much of the time
          life just won't be
          the way you want it to be.

Every thing changes.
Pain is the result of clinging
in an attempt to resist
change.

When we comprehend the process
of suffering,
how we do suffering,
we are free to choose not to do it anymore.

To do anything
there must be the willingness
to do it.
Achievement
is commensurate with
effort;
effort is commensurate
with willingness.

Remember: We have no control over what we
get, only over what we do.

The only thing standing in your way
is the "what" you have decided is
in your way,
the "what" you're thinking is in your way,
the "what" you're seeing as in your way,
the "what" you believe is in your way.

If you didn't experience it as an
///// obstacle,
would it be one?

What are you experiencing as an obstacle in your life?

What belief are you clinging to about how life should be that makes this obstacle an obstacle?

What have you already decided about this obstacle (its future, how things are going to be, etc.)?

What are you getting out of having this obstacle in your life (positive and negative)?

What would happen if you let go?

This is a formula you can use to work on any problem.

110.

given a choice (which we always have),
we will almost always choose our
   feelings
   over
what we "know" is best for us.

For instance:
              I want to quit smoking,
but it feels so uncomfortable when I stop;
              I want to meditate,
but my thoughts drive me crazy when I sit;
       I want not to drink alcohol (or eat meat),
but my friends put so much pressure on me.

   It's good to remember
      that no one
      ever died
         of
   uncomfortable.

We always do
what we are willing to do.

We always have a choice. "I can't,"
is what we say in order to keep pretending
that we're not responsible.

Here is a definition of perfect trust:
People will always do what they want to do.

When we start to use words like "I choose"
and "I choose not" we start to be
honest with ourselves.

Think of three things you can't do.
(It's helpful to keep it in the realm of
possibility — not "I can't flap my wings
and fly!")

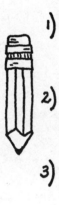

1)

2)

3)

Now repeat the same three with
" I won't... "

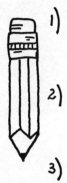

1)

2)

3)

Now, the same three with
" I choose not..."

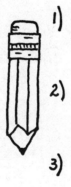

1)

2)

3)

This is your best opportunity...

There will never be a better
opportunity than this one. No better
time, no better place, no better
circumstances.

Right here,
Right now.
Right this minute.

If it's really a hard time for you,
you're closest to the truth.

When you're drowning,
it is your very best opportunity
to learn to swim!

The reason that it is your best opportunity
is that there is nothing else on your
mind, nothing you need to get
done first. It is your first priority.

And we always do what is truly
our first priority.

Do not be confused by what you say
is most important to you.

Watch what you do.

What you do
is what is most important to you.

If the answers were in
the places you've been looking...

you would already
have found them...

Obviously,
  if the way you've been doing it worked,
  you wouldn't still be looking for answers.
And yet our fear
        of doing it differently,
        of facing the unknown,
        of going against society,
        of questioning our conditioning,
            is so great
                that we continue to follow
    the same patterns over and over,
even when we know full-well
        that they lead to unhappiness.

We continue to choose our beliefs
over our experience.

A rat in a laboratory learns very quickly
not to go down the tunnel if there is
no longer cheese at the other end.
A human being will continue to go down the
tunnel even though there's never been
any cheese at the end!

We can certainly learn as much from what we
reject
as from what we
accept.

What you're pushing away
may contain exactly the clue
that you've been looking for.

In other words...

If the answers you're seeking
were in the places you've been looking
you would already have found them.

Our defenses
don't prove that we need to be defended,
they prove that we're not taking care
of ourselves.
They indicate that we're not doing the love,
compassion and care that we need.

We feel vulnerable because we don't trust
that the love, wisdom and compassion
we need
will be there when we need it.

We have identified with a small,
separate self who suffers and we
have forgotten that that's not
who we really are.

That which you are seeking
is causing you to seek.

As long as you're looking outward,
you're looking in
the wrong direction.

This is an equal opportunity life.

We each have all we need
                    each moment.

We can choose
to let go

and be free...

When we begin to take responsibility
we are like the conductor for a large
symphony orchestra. The various instruments
are the parts of us, all our ways
of being, needs, wants, moods, etc.
The symphony is our life.
Sometimes we see parts of ourselves
that we decide are bad, wrong, undesirable
and that should be gotten rid of.
It's like having the string sections
hear the drums or cymbals and say,
"Oh, no, that sounds awful. We've got
to get rid of all that noise!
All we need are stringed instruments
because they sound so beautiful."
(Beauty, clearly, being in the ear of the beholder.)
An orchestra made up of only stringed
instruments would be lacking, incomplete.
It could make many beautiful sounds,
and it couldn't make all music.

Only one section of instruments could hate
another. The conductor can hear the
beauty in all and knows that each is
essential to the whole.

When we need a drum roll in life,
a violin simply won't do!

125.

We've been taught to believe
that we need to hold onto this
                    and push that away.
                    And that is simply not true.

It's like being taught to believe
that half the orchestra can play more
beautiful music than the whole orchestra.
When you hear all the instruments playing
    together in harmony you will be most
        grateful that you were unable to
        get rid of even the smallest,
    apparently most insignificant, piece.

Your life can be different
in any moment you choose
to change your choices.

When we're too busy to pay attention,
we're choosing ignorance.

Practice ...*

If you want to call yourself a tennis player,
   you can borrow a racquet and a few balls
   and go out and hit the balls with
            the racquet.
If you want to play tennis, you buy a
   racquet, take some lessons and play when
            you have time.
If you want to play tennis well, you find
   a teacher, you take lessons, you practice
            and you play regularly.
If you want to be a master tennis player,
   you find a teacher, absorb every bit
   of guidance, you practice every possible
   moment and your entire life is devoted
            to your training.

            Our lives are as they are
            because we choose them.
We want to say, "Oh, but I don't have time
   to pay attention," "I'm too busy to be
   aware." That's ok. It's just good to
know who is making the decisions.
   Your life is not beyond you.

* and remember, only practice when
   you want to, not because you "should.

Not to worry...

There is nothing to worry about.
     No urgency.
     No hurry.
When you're tired enough of struggling,
          of suffering, of being unhappy,
               you'll stop.

One day you'll be different.
It will be like walking around a corner
               or turning on a light.
     Everything will be different
     and nothing will have changed.

Someday   you'll do it.
     When you're tired enough
          of struggling
          of suffering
          of being unhappy...

Or you could just do it now.

How

How do you do it?
What does how mean?
How do you let go?
How do you accept?
How do you stop suffering?
How do you find compassion?
How do you learn to love?
          HOW ????????

How did you learn to walk?
Did someone tell you about the
    muscles and bones and tendons and
    blood in your legs?
Did someone explain how the muscles
    in your stomach and arms and legs
    would all work together, and how
    messages come into and out of
    your brain and how...

Or did you one day decide that you
wanted to get up and go so badly
that nothing could stop you. Not
fear or pain or ignorance or
insecurity. You wanted to walk and
the only way to do it was get up and do it.

That's how.

(continued on page 1)

NOTES